BQ.

AsParagUs

Author: Thea Spierings
Editing: Jessica Verbruggen, Loes Verhoeven, Désirée Verkaar
Final editing: Anda Schippers
Art direction/vormgeving: Kirsti Alink
Photography: Mark van Stokkom, Food4eyes.com
Styling: Moniek Visser
With thanx to: De Bijenkorf, Dille&Kamille Arnhem, HEMA, IKEA BV,
Vivre landelijk wonen Nijmegen, Zus&Zo.
Publisher: Pieter Harts

© English edition: Miller Books
email: info@miller-books.com
www.miller-books.com
1st printing 2008

ISBN 978-90-8724-046-2

Foreword

Asparagus has been eaten for thousands of years. The spears were regarded as food of the gods, as an aphrodisiac or as having healing properties.
Nowadays we eat them simply because they taste good. Straight out of the ground into the pan: when it's fresh, asparagus is beyond compare.

This cookbook contains numerous traditional recipes as well as new ones. Asparagus plays the starring role in all of them. After all, home-grown asparagus is only available for two months per year. In that short time, we should use it as often as possible!

Contents

White Asparagus

Well before the spring sun has risen, hundreds of people, stooping forward, move across bare fields. Every few meters, little star-shaped cracks appear in the cool earth. The treasure-diggers wipe the sand away carefully, then, using a long knife, unearth the exquisite asparagus.

The asparagus harvest has a magical quality about it. The vegetable has been eaten for centuries and is still harvested in the same way: by hand. They have to be taken out of the ground at daybreak as sunlight colours the ivory white spears from violet to clear green within a few hours. If the young shoots are given the chance, they will grow into beautiful, delicate, foliage that can be used in bouquets. By digging up the asparagus plants before they appear above ground, their creamy white colour and subtle taste is preserved.

The young asparagus plants need four years of tender loving care before they can be harvested. First, the precious seed grows on a seedbed and then for two years in the asparagus field. In May of the fourth year, growers can cut some new shoots, but after a few weeks, the plants need to rest once more. In the fifth spring, their patience will be rewarded. During a whole season, they can harvest what they entrusted to the earth.

Traditionally, the asparagus harvest ends on 24 June, the feast day of St. John the Baptist. From then onwards, the growers allow the shoots to grow into shrubs that collect solar energy during the summer for the next asparagus season.

Whoever yields to the temptation and continues cutting, can expect a reduced crop in the following year. Asparagus can be harvested from the same field for eight to ten years. From then on, the quantity of spears will decrease.

'Asparagos'

White gold, king of vegetables... the epithets of the asparagus fire the imagination. For centuries, the vegetable has been seen as food of the gods, an aphrodisiac or as having medicinal qualities. After his death, the Egyptian pharaoh Sakkara (circa. 3000 BC) was given sheafs of asparagus on his journey to eternal life. On the wall paintings in his tomb, his subjects give him not only peaches and figs but also asparagus to take to the underworld.

The ancient Greeks collected wild asparagus from the countryside and gave the vegetable the name 'asparagos' which means the 'unsown'. The first to cultivate the plant themselves were the Romans. Researchers have

found Roman documents from 2000 BC that describe the cultivation of asparagus and also extensive meals made with this vegetable. There are even recipes from that time, such as a kind of frittata with asparagus, goat cheese and parsley. The vegetable was usually cooked for a short while until it was still firm. Emperor Augustus had a saying about this: when something had to be done quickly, he spoke the legendary words 'velocius quam asparagi conquantur' meaning 'quicker than the time asparagus needs to cook'. Before the Romans started to cultivate asparagus, they thought that the spears emerged from ram's horns buried underground.

Only in the seventeenth century did asparagus make an appearance in Western Europe. The Sun King, Louis XIV of France, was a great connoisseur of asparagus. In addition to his vegetable gardens and orchards, he had greenhouses built in which the asparagus were ready to be harvested in March. The Dutch also started to eat so-called 'aspergies' around that time. The book 'De Verstandige Kock of Sorgvuldige Huyshoudster' (The Sensible Cook or Careful Housekeeper) from 1668, gives the following recipe: 'asparagus are only cooked, not too soft, and then eaten with oil, vinegar and pepper, or otherwise with butter and grated nutmeg'.

White, green, and violet

Cooked asparagus with butter sauce; that is how the Dutch, Belgians, Germans and Americans like them the best. Italians, however, prefer the sturdy green asparagus. In China, the largest asparagus producer in

Popular: asparagus with butter

The most popular asparagus recipe in Holland is asparagus with butter: cooked asparagus with slices of ham and hard boiled eggs, melted butter and parsley (see the recipes in the inset). A glass of dry white Alsace wine goes well with this classic recipe. If you want to be dignified and apply the rules of etiquette, you hold the bottom part of the asparagus in the left hand, 'drag' it through the butter and then bring it to your mouth, the crown supported by your fork.

Sensually stimulating

For centuries, the asparagus was seen as an aphrodisiac. The ancient Egyptians used raw asparagus as such and eighteenth century doctors prescribed it as a remedy for impotence. Today, the sensually stimulating effect is due to the shape and the method of eating it with the fingers, when the asparagus slowly glides into the mouth glistening with butter. Consequently, eating asparagus was seen as very unladylike in the Victorian era. In his book of etiquette, Pierre Louys warns young girls: 'never eat asparagus when a charming young man is looking at you.'

Many healing properties have been ascribed to the asparagus. The scientific name 'Asparagus Officinalis' was given for a reason: the addition roughly means 'from the pharmacy'. Asparagus was thought to be good for kidneys, bladder, and heart and help against toothache, bee stings, and jaundice. These particular claims have never been proven but it is certain that the asparagus has few calories and a lot of nutrients: vitamin B and C, protein, fibre, and minerals such as potassium and iron.

the world, they eat white as well as green asparagus.

Both kinds are from the same plant: the difference is in the way of growing and harvesting. The white asparagus is carefully covered with an earthen hillock, so it will never come in contact with sunlight. The green asparagus is allowed to grow above the earth and is cut when it is about twenty five centimetres high. Sunlight allows chlorophyll to develop in the shoot and thus gives the plant its green colour.

The taste of the green asparagus is slightly stronger, more pungent and bitter. However, the typical asparagus taste, which originates from asparagus acid, is less strong in the green version. It does have one big advantage though: you can save on time-consuming peeling as shoots grown above ground have a thinner skin.

The quantities of each are, world-wide, more or less the same; 51% of all cultivated asparagus is white and 48% green. The remaining one per cent is made up of the violet-coloured French asparagus. These vary in colour from light-pink to violet or purple, sometimes with a partly white stalk. They are harvested when they are about 3 centimetres high and their taste lies somewhere between that of the white and the green varieties.

Perfection

The asparagus has almost thirty different quality classes and with that beats all other vegetables. The most important classification of the European Union is in the classes Extra, I, and II. The first is made up of the real white gold; perfectly white, straight and undamaged. Class II also meets the strict demands; it

may not look as perfect but it tastes just as good (and is less expensive).

Strange smell

After eating asparagus, a person's urine smells strange; this is caused by the release of sulphurous chemicals when the asparagus acid is broken down. Some people may be more bothered by the smell than others. This is not because they do not have the enzymes necessary for breaking down the chemical (as was once thought), but because not everybody can smell the odour. Everyone produces it, but it is genetically determined if you can smell it or not.

Producers

Traditionally, almost all of Britain's asparagus farmers came from the Vale of Evesham in Worcestershire. Nowadays, there are also major producers in Kent, Lincolnshire and Cambridgeshire.

Asparagus sold out of season usually comes from South and Central America or South Africa. Asparagus is also grown, on a smaller scale, in greenhouses. Wild asparagus can sometimes be found in certain places in coastal dunes. They have thin, horizontal, stems and poisonous dark-red berries in autumn.

Buying and preparing asparagus

Whatever the colour of asparagus, freshness is important: straight from the land onto your plate is best. When buying, take care that they do not look dried out. A trick of the trade for white asparagus is to rub two together; if they are fresh, they will make a squeaking or creaking noise. Rolled in a moist cloth, they will stay fresh in the refrigerator for two to three days.

Peeling: Peeling white asparagus is a precise job. There is nothing as annoying as bits of hard, woody, asparagus skin that have been missed. Peel the asparagus just before cooking and put the peeled asparagus in a moist cloth to stop them drying out. Start peeling just under the crown and peel from top to bottom with an asparagus peeler or thin peeler, do this in overlapping strokes so that not a single flake is forgotten. Cut off the woody tip.

Cooking: Although it might be more work, the following method does lead to an improved taste.

Make a concentrated stock from the skins and cook the asparagus in this. Put the skins and the bits that were cut off in the pan together with cold water and a knob of butter and bring it almost to the boil. Simmer for about ten minutes and then sieve the liquid. Lay the asparagus next to each other in a pan and pour the asparagus stock over them, then simmer for ten to fifteen minutes over a low flame. The concentrated stock should not cook as the asparagus will then become bitter. The preparation time depends on the thickness of the asparagus; they are ready if you can easily prick your fork in the bottom, but still feel solid. Take them out of the liquid (a perfect base for soups and sauces!) and let them drain on a clean tea towel. You can also cook them for five minutes and then take the pan off the heat source, allowing them to cook in the hot liquid for a further 15 minutes. In this way, you will have time to prepare the rest of the recipe – or to enjoy a first course.

About this book

The asparagus tastes wonderful with butter sauce, but it has so much more to offer. It is perfect for soups and salads and great when combined with other ingredients for meat, fish or vegetarian meals. You will find eighty original dishes in this book with the king of vegetables as the main focus of attention. All recipes are intended for four people. Allow yourself to be inspired and discover how versatile white gold truly is.

Traditional recipe

Asparagus Polonaise (Poland)

1kg asparagus, cooked but still firm
4 hard boiled eggs, finely mashed
1 tablespoonful parsley, chopped
Bread crumbs made from 1 slice of white bread

Lay the asparagus in a baking dish and sprinkle the crowns with the hard boiled eggs, parsley, and the bread crumbs.
Cook au gratin in the oven

Traditional recipe

Asparagus à la Milanaise (Italy)

1kg asparagus, cooked but
still firm
100g cheese, grated
100g butter, melted

Lay the asparagus in a baking dish.
Sprinkle the crowns
with cheese and pour the butter over the
dish
Cook au gratin in the oven.

Kitchen accessories

Asparagus peelers: these come in all shapes and sizes, from simple peelers to appliances with which to remove the tough layer of the asparagus by turning a handle – or even by pressing a button.

The spears can remain upright in a high, narrow asparagus pot. The crowns stay above water so they are steamed and not cooked to a pulp.

There are also various types of asparagus tongs. They have been designed in such a way that you can pick up the delicate asparagus spears without damaging them.

An asparagus dish has ridges on the bottom for the vegetables to lie on, or a perforated bottom with a drainer. In this way, the liquid leaking from the asparagus after cooking will not get onto the plate.

Traditional recipe

Buttered asparagus (The Netherlands)

2kg asparagus, cooked but still firm, cut into equal lengths.
8 eggs, hard boiled, cut in halves.
400g ham
1 bunch of parsley, chopped finely,
Nutmeg powder
200g butter, melted

Portion the asparagus on to four plates. Lay all the crowns in the same direction. Place the eggs next to them. Lay the slices of ham over the bottom of the asparagus. Sprinkle with nutmeg as desired. Garnish with the parsley and serve with butter.

Starters

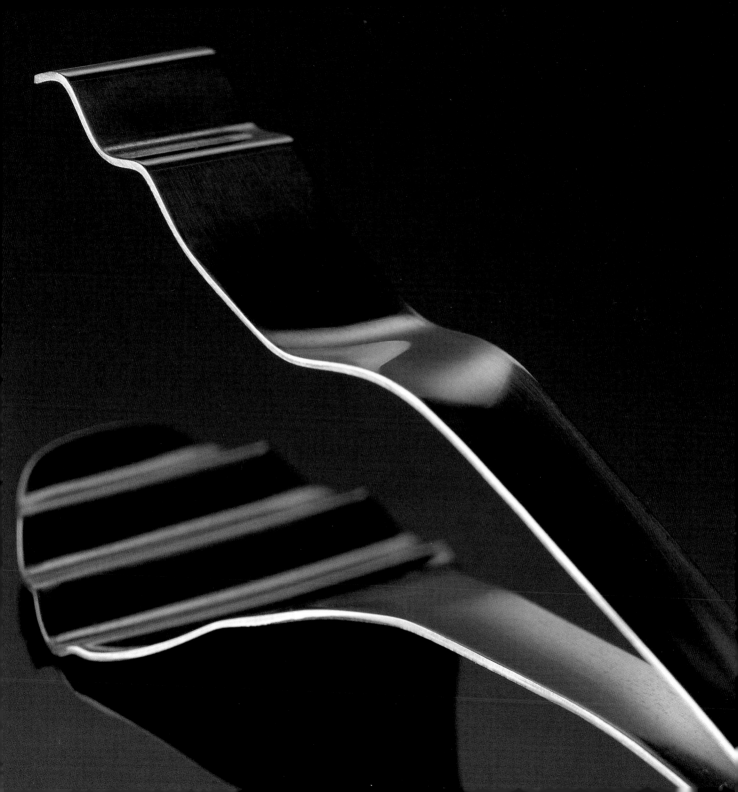

Asparagus with tomatoes and marsh samphire

1kg asparagus, cooked,
in lengths of 5 cm
4 large tomatoes, skinned and
cut into eighths
knob of butter
1 tbs white wine
1 tbs cooking cream
100g marsh samphire
salt

1. Melt the butter. Simmer the tomato and the asparagus briefly in the butter.
2. Take the asparagus and tomato out of the pan. Add the wine and the cream to the pan and reduce. Flavour with salt.
3. Return the asparagus and tomato to the sauce and allow to warm.
4. Bring water to the boil in another pan and immerse the marsh samphire. Remove immediately and drain in a colander.
5. Portion the asparagus and tomatoes on to four plates and arrange the marsh samphire around them.

Scrambled eggs with smoked salmon and asparagus

6 eggs
4 asparagus spears,
cooked, in lengths
100g smoked salmon, in strips
1 tbs cooking cream
2 tbs parsley, chopped finely
salt and pepper

1 Loosely beat the eggs with the cream and a little salt and pepper.
2 Scramble the eggs in a pan with a knob of butter till they are almost set.
3 Add the salmon and asparagus and fry them together for a minute.
4 Portion on to four plates and garnish with parsley.
5 Serve with toasted bread.

Sweetbread, stir-fried asparagus and Madeira sauce

400g sweetbread (cleaned) in slices of 1cm
500g asparagus in strips of 4cm
1 tbs flour
salt and pepper
Butter for frying

For the sauce:
½ onion, finely sliced.
½ large carrot, finely sliced
¼ stick of celery
380ml concentrated stock
200ml Madeira
200ml cream
1 tbs olive oil
pepper and salt

1 To make the sauce; fry the onion, carrot, and celery gently in oil. Add the stock, Madeira and cream and simmer for half an hour.
2 Strain the sauce and flavour with salt and pepper. Set apart or reduce further if you want a thicker sauce.
3 Sprinkle pepper and salt over the sweetbread.
4 Let it brown nicely in butter for 2 minutes.
5 Stir-fry the asparagus until completely cooked.
6 Warm up the sauce if necessary. Portion the asparagus on to four plates, lay the slices of sweetbread on top and add the sauce.

Wok asparagus with pak-choi and red pepper

500g asparagus, cooked,
in lengths of 5cm
2 heads of pak-choi
in large pieces
1 red pepper, halved
lengthwise with seeds removed
1 tbs maize oil
1 tbs sesame oil
1 tbs soy sauce
salt

1 Heat the two types of oil in the wok and stir-fry the asparagus in two minutes.
2 Add the pak-choi and the pepper and fry together for another minute.
3 Pour the soy sauce into the wok and warm it up. Flavour with salt.

Fried asparagus with sherry and goat cheese

6 asparagus spears, peeled,
cut at an angle, in small pieces
6 green asparagus spears,
with the hard underside
removed
1 tbs butter
1 glass of sherry
100g crème fraîche
4 small slices of goats cheese
pepper and salt

1 Fry the asparagus in butter until it begins to brown.
2 Take the pan off the heat and add the sherry and crème fraîche. Stir well and return to the heat.
3 Reduce the mixture to half and flavour with salt and pepper
4 Portion on to four plates. Lay the slices of goats cheese on the plates and place under the grill until they are nicely browned.

Asparagus with warm salmon and white wine sauce

14 asparagus spears, cooked but still firm
200g fresh salmon, in thin slices
3 tbs cooking cream
1 tbs white wine
3 tbs stock
8 blades of chives
salt

1 To make the sauce, reduce the cream, wine and stock to half.
2 Cut 2 asparagus in small pieces and add them to the reduced sauce.
3 Purée the sauce with a hand-held blender.
4 Place 3 spears of asparagus on each plate. Arrange the pieces of salmon over the ends of the asparagus. Place under the grill and leave long enough for the salmon to become warm but remain pink on the inside.
5 Pour a little sauce next to the salmon and garnish with chives.

Asparagus with frothy oyster sauce

12 asparagus spears,
cooked but still firm
4 large oysters, taken out of
the shell, byssus removed,
in thin slices
3 tbs white wine
4 tbs asparagus stock
(see introduction to this book)
1 tbs cooking cream
100g rocket
salt

1 To make the sauce, reduce the white wine and the asparagus stock to half.
2 Beat the cooking cream through the stock till it becomes a frothy mass.
3 Stir the oysters through the sauce and flavour with salt.
4 Portion the asparagus on to four plates and pour the sauce over the ends of the asparagus.
5 Garnish with rocket.

Salmon tartare with asparagus and sherry dressing

100g fresh salmon, in cubes
100g smoked salmon,
in small pieces
1 shallot, finely shredded
Juice of ½ lemon
3 asparagus spears,
in small pieces
100g mixed lettuce,
torn into big pieces

For the sherry dressing:
1 tsp mustard
1 tsp honey
2 tbs stock
1 egg yolk
1 teaspoon white wine vinegar
2 tbs sherry
3dl maize oil

1   Mix the raw and the smoked salmon with the shallot, the lemon juice and 2 of the asparagus.
2   Use a cutter to make 4 nice rounds.
3   To make the sherry dressing; mix the mustard, honey, stock, egg yolk, vinegar and sherry with a hand blender. Add the maize oil till the dressing thickens.
4   Portion the salad on to four plates, put the salmon tartare in the middle and dot the dressing around it.
5   Garnish with the rest of the asparagus.

Scallops with stir-fry spinach and asparagus

12 scallops
100g spinach
4 asparagus spears,
peeled, cut at an angle
1 tbs balsamic vinegar
Sea salt

For the antiboise
(Antibes sauce):
3 Pomadoro tomatoes,
skinned, without seeds,
in cubes
1 garlic clove, chopped
10 basil leaves, in thin strips
50ml olive oil

1. Mix the ingredients for the antiboise.
2. Stir-fry the asparagus till they are cooked, but still firm.
3. Stir-fry the spinach in another pan.
4. Brown the scallops slightly on both sides.
5. Portion the spinach on to four plates, place in the middle, and put the asparagus on top.
6. Lay 3 scallops on top of this.
7. Spoon the antiboise around it, then drizzle a little balsamic vinegar over it and sprinkle with sea salt.

Tuna tartare

200g fresh tuna fillet in
small cubes
1 shallot, finely chopped
4 asparagus spears,
peeled, in cubes
salt and pepper

1 Mix the tuna with the shallot and half of the asparagus.
2 Flavour with pepper and salt
3 Use a cutter to make four rounds. Garnish with the remaining
   asparagus and alfalfa sprouts.

*Tip: tastes great together with the antiboise (see previous recipe
or basil oil.*

Soup

Asparagus soup with minced veal

4 asparagus spears, peeled
(keep the skins) and
cut at an angle
200g minced veal
1l beef stock
1 egg yolk
4 sprigs of parsley,
finely chopped
salt and pepper

1 Warm the stock and add the asparagus skins. Allow to stew for 15 minutes.
2 Sieve the stock and put it back on the heat source. Bring to the boil again.
3 Mix the minced veal with the egg yolk and a little pepper and salt and shape nicely into balls. Put them in the stock and let the soup simmer for another 5 minutes.
4 Portion the soup into four bowls and garnish with parsley.

Asparagus-pea soup with Parmesan cheese

4 asparagus spears, in pieces,
cut at an angle
500g peas, fresh or frozen
1l vegetable stock
2 tbs cooking cream
100g shaved Parmesan
(use cheese grater to make
shavings)

1. Heat up the stock and cook the peas in it.
2. Use the hand blender to purée the peas.
3. Stir in the cream and warm the soup up again. Add the asparagus and let the soup simmer for 3 minutes.
4. Portion the soup into four bowls. Sprinkle the cheese over the soup.

Asparagus stock with poached quails' eggs

1l chicken stock
4 asparagus spears, peeled
and cut at an angle
12 fresh quails' eggs
1 tsp vinegar
2 tbs chervil, chopped
salt

1 Poach the eggs by bringing water to the boil in a saucepan and adding salt and pepper. Turn off the heat, break an egg above a spoon and let it glide into the hot water. Poach 4 eggs collectively in 2 minutes. Heat the water each time before you poach the next portion. Carefully scoop the eggs out of the water with a skimmer.
3 Heat the stock, add the asparagus, and simmer for 5 minutes.
3 Portion the soup into four bowls and share out the eggs. Garnish with chervil.

Tip: To poach the eggs properly, make sure they are very fresh.

Traditional asparagus soup

500g asparagus, peeled,
(keep the skins) and
cut at an angle
1l beef stock
40g butter
35g flour
2dl cream
salt

1 Stew the asparagus skins in the stock for 10 minutes; then sieve the stock and let it cool.
2 Make a roux by melting the butter and stirring in the flour and allow to gently simmer.
3 Add a soup spoon of cold stock and stir till the flour is mixed with the stock. Add some more stock and carry on in this way till all the stock has been used.
4 Bring the soup to the boil and sieve it to remove any possible lumps.
5 Heat the soup again, add the cream and the pieces of asparagus and simmer till the asparagus is cooked but still firm.
6 Flavour with salt.

Cappuccino of asparagus and shrimps

1l vegetable stock
4 asparagus spears, peeled,
in pieces
200g shrimps
200ml warm milk,
whisked into a froth

1 Heat the stock and add the asparagus. Simmer for 3 minutes.
2 Stir in the shrimps.
3 Fill four cappuccino cups with the soup and spoon the milk on top.

Vegetable stock with scampi, asparagus, and lemon balm

1l vegetable stock
16 scampi, peeled and with
the intestinal track removed
4 asparagus spears, peeled
and cut at an angle
3 sprigs of lemon balm
1 tbs lemon balm leaves,
finely cut
pepper and salt

1 Heat the vegetable stock and the sprigs of lemon balm and simmer for 5 minutes.
2 Sieve the vegetable stock and replace on the heat source. Add the pieces of asparagus and simmer for 3 minutes.
3 Add the scampi and simmer for 30 seconds. Taste and add pepper and salt if necessary.
4 Portion the soup into the bowls and garnish with the finely cut lemon balm leaves.

Asparagus chicken soup

1l substantial chicken stock
200g fillet of chicken,
in small pieces
4 asparagus spears, peeled,
in pieces cut at an angle
½ leek, in thin slices

1 Bring the stock to the boil and add the asparagus. Simmer for 4 minutes.
2 Add the chicken, and cook for about 5 minutes.
3 Add the leek and cook for a minute. Serve in four deep soup plates.

White and green asparagus soup

1l vegetable stock
4 white asparagus spears,
peeled (keep the skins)
in large pieces
4 green asparagus spears,
hard underside removed,
in large pieces
1 sprig of celery,
finely chopped

1 Heat the stock, add the asparagus skins and simmer for 10 minutes. Sieve the stock.
2 Bring to the boil again and add the pieces of white asparagus. Add the green asparagus after three minutes. Simmer for three minutes.
3 Garnish the soup with the celery

Clear asparagus soup with scallops

1l vegetable stock
4 asparagus spears, peeled
(keep the skins), in pieces
4 scallops, in thin slices
1 tbs cress

1 Lay the slices of scallop in four deep plates.
2 Heat the stock and stew the asparagus skins for 10 minutes. Sieve and heat again till the stock is very hot.
3 Add the asparagus and simmer for 4 minutes.
4 Spoon the hot stock onto the scallops and garnish with cress.

Cappuccino with asparagus, eel, and broccoli

1l clear stock
4 asparagus spears, peeled,
in thin slices
50g smoked eel, in thin slices
4 small broccoli flowerets,
cooked for 1 minute
in boiling water
200ml warm milk,
whisked into a froth

1 Heat the stock and add the slices of asparagus.
2 Simmer for 1 minute.
3 Portion the stock into four bowl or cappuccino cups and add the eel and broccoli.
4 Spoon the frothy milk over the stock.

Salads

Asparagus salad with quail and red wine sauce

4 quails; breasts and legs
500g asparagus, cooked but
still firm, in pieces
2 tbs butter
1 tbs herbs (parsley, chervil,
chives), finely chopped
½ head frisée lettuce,
torn into large pieces
1 spring onion, shredded finely
salt and pepper

For the vinaigrette:
1 tbs walnut oil
1 tbs stock
1 tbs

For the sauce:
½ onion, cut fine
½ large carrot, cut fine
¼ stick of blanched celery,
cut fine
380ml concentrated stock
200ml red wine
200ml cream
1 tbs olive oil

1 To make the sauce, gently fry the onion, carrot, and celery. Add the concentrated stock, red wine and cream. Simmer for 10 minutes.
2 Sprinkle the quail legs with a little salt and brown in the butter. Add the red wine sauce until they are covered and simmer for 20 minutes.
3 Sieve the sauce and cook till reduced by half. Flavour with salt and pepper.
4 Mix the ingredients for the vinaigrette. Mix herbs, lettuce and vinaigrette and portion on to four plates.
5 Add the asparagus to the salad.
6 Brown the breasts and cut into thin slices. Lay them over the salad in a fan shape. Add the legs. Garnish with the spring onion.
7 Pour the sauce around the salad.

Asparagus salad with truffle dressing

500g asparagus, cooked,
cut at angle
1 egg, hard boiled,
mashed finely
50g truffles (fresh or otherwise),
one half in large pieces, the
other half finely shaved
(use a cheese grater)

For the dressing:
2 tbs white wine vinegar
1 tbs truffle oil
1 tbs maize oil
1 tbs stock
1 tsp red wine vinegar
salt

1   Blend all the ingredients for the dressing and flavour with salt.
2   Add the egg and the large pieces of truffle. Warm the dressing, but do not allow to boil.
3   Portion the asparagus out on to four plates and sprinkle with the dressing. Carefully add the egg and the truffle.
4   Sprinkle the shaved truffle over the salad.

Green chicken salad with raspberry dressing

400g smoked chicken fillet
in thin slices
500g asparagus, cooked,
but still firm, sliced at an angle
100g rocket,
chopped coarsely

For the dressing:
25g raspberries (set aside
12 for garnishing)
1 tbs vegetable stock
1 tsp raspberry vinegar
1 tsp honey
4 tbs crème fraîche

1 Mix the ingredients for the dressing with the hand blender.
2 Mix the rocket with the asparagus and portion on to four plates
4 Spoon the dressing around the salad.
   Garnish with the raspberries.

Turkey asparagus salad
with apple dressing

500g asparagus, cooked but
still firm, sliced at an angle
400g turkey fillet,
fried and sliced
100g mixed salad,
torn in pieces
1 firm apple, in small slices
1 red onion, in half-rings
salt

For the dressing:
1 apple in pieces
1 tbs maize oil
1 tbs stock
1 tsp apple vinegar
1 tsp honey
Salt

1   Mix the ingredients for the dressing with the hand-held blender till the apple is very fine. Season with salt.
2   Portion the salad on to four plates. Lay the asparagus on to the salad, then the slices of turkey fillet, the slices of apple and the onion rings.
3   Pour the dressing over the salad.

Herring asparagus salad with dill oil

2 herrings, in pieces
500g asparagus
cooked, in pieces
50g almond shavings, roasted

For the dressing:
4 tbs olive oil
½ bunch of dill
Salt

1 Make a smooth dressing by blending the oil and the dill together with the hand-held blender. Add salt to taste.
2 Portion the asparagus on to four plates. Lay the pieces of herring on top.
3 Sprinkle with almond shavings and with dill oil.

Pasta salad with white and green asparagus

150g tagliatelle, al dente
250g white asparagus,
cooked but still firm, in pieces
250g green asparagus,
cooked but still firm, in pieces
2 tbs parsley, chopped
1 roasted sweet pepper*
in slices
1 punnet of watercress, cut

For the dressing:
1 tbs grated lemon rind
2 tbs olive oil
Juice of 1 lemon
1 tsp honey
salt and pepper

1 Mix the ingredients for the dressing, add salt and pepper to taste.
2 Mix the pasta with the asparagus, the parsley and the dressing
3 Portion on to four plates. Garnish with slices of sweet pepper and cress.

*Put a sweet pepper on a piece of aluminium foil in an oven at 200 to 220°C (392°F to 428°F). Take it out of the oven when the skin is scorched (after about 30 minutes) If necessary, turn the sweet pepper halfway through the cooking time. Fold the foil closed and let it rest for 5 minutes. Pull the skin off the sweet pepper and remove the seeds.

Lamb tongue and asparagus salad with Marsala sauce

4 lamb tongues, cooked for
20 minutes, in thin slices
500g asparagus, cooked
but still firm, in pieces
100g lamb's lettuce

For the sauce:
½ onion, finely cut
½ large carrot, finely cut
¼ blanched celery, finely cut
380ml concentrated stock
200ml Marsala
200ml cream
1 tbs olive oil
pepper and salt

1 To make the sauce, fry the onion, carrot, and blanched celery gently in the olive oil. Add the stock, the Marsala, and the cream and simmer for half an hour. Strain the sauce and flavour with salt and pepper. Keep separate or reduce if you want a thicker sauce.

2 Place the lamb's lettuce on the plates, then arrange the asparagus and put the tongues next to them. Pour the sauce over the dish.

Asparagus and artichoke salad

500g asparagus, cooked
but still firm, in pieces
100g French beans,
cooked but still firm
1 red sweet pepper, in pieces,
cut at an angle
50g chestnut mushrooms,
fried in 1 tbs olive oil, halved
5 tinned artichoke hearts,
cut in four parts
1 punnet of cress

For the dressing:
1 clove of garlic
2 tbs olive oil
2 tbs lemon juice
2 tbs basil
salt

1 Put all the ingredients for the dressing together and purée them with the hand-held blender
2 Place the asparagus, French beans, paprika, mushrooms, and artichoke hearts in a bowl and mix with the dressing.
3 Portion the salad on to four plates and sprinkle lightly with cress.

Asparagus salad with feta and sun-dried tomatoes

500g asparagus,
cooked, in pieces
4 tbs olive oil
1 tsp balsamic vinegar
100g feta, crumbled
1 tbs sun-dried tomatoes
in slices
1 spring onion, in thin rings
1 tbs pine nuts, roasted
salt

1   Beat the balsamic vinegar with the oil, flavour with a little salt and mix with the asparagus.
2   Portion on to four plates. Then add the feta, tomato, spring onion, and the pine nuts.

Grilled asparagus salad with Parma ham and pears

500g asparagus, in pieces
12 slices of Parma ham
2 eating pears (Conference),
peeled, core taken out,
in eight pieces
½ head frisée lettuce,
in pieces

For the dressing:
1 tbs champagne vinegar
1 tsp mustard
4 tbs olive oil
1 tsp honey
salt

1 Blend the ingredients for the dressing and flavour with salt.
2 Toss the dressing with the frisée lettuce and portion on to four plates.
3 Grill the asparagus for a few minutes on a grill plate till they turn nicely brown.
4 Fry the Parma ham in a dry frying pan till it is crispy and let it dry on kitchen paper.
5 Place the pears on the grill till they are also nicely brown.
6 Divide the asparagus, the pears, and the ham over the salad.

Asparagus and chicory salad with shrimps and lemon dressing

20 chicory leaves
500g asparagus, cooked
but still firm, in small cubes
100g shrimps
50g marsh samphire,
immersed for a short while
in boiling water, then rinsed
with cold water immediately
afterwards

For the dressing:
4 tbs maize oil
1 tsp white wine vinegar
Juice from 1 lemon
1 tsp mustard
1 egg yolk
1 tsp honey
1 tbs stock
salt

1   Put the ingredients for the dressing in a bowl (with the exception of the oil) and mix well.
2   Beat the oil slowly, drop for drop, through the dressing until it binds. Flavour with salt.
3   Portion chicory leaves on to the plates. Place the shrimps in the middle with the asparagus cubes on top. Sprinkle with the dressing and garnish with the marsh samphire.

Seafood salad with stir-fried asparagus

500g fresh mussels,
washed and checked
250g green asparagus,
cooked but still firm, in pieces
100g white asparagus,
cooked but still firm, in pieces
100g shrimps
½ red pepper, in thin rings
½ leek, in thin rings
1 tbs oil

Cooking liquid for the mussels:
100ml white wine
½ leek, finely cut
½ large carrot, finely cut
½ onion
1 bay leaf
pepper and salt

For the dressing:
1 tsp lemon juice
1 tsp mustard
4 tbs maize oil
salt and pepper

1 Put all the ingredients for the cooking liquid in a pan and add the mussels. Put the lid on the pan and cook until the mussels open. Shake them once or twice.
2 Strain the contents of the pan and remove the mussels (keep them in their shells). Keep the liquid.
3 Mix the dressing with 2 tbs mussel liquid, the lemon juice, and the mustard and then stir in the oil slowly. Flavour with salt and pepper.
4 For the salad, stir-fry the red pepper, the leek, and the asparagus for about 1 minute in the oil.
5 Portion the mixture on to four plates and add the mussels.
6 Spoon the shrimps on to the plates and pour the dressing over them.

Green bean and asparagus salad with grated goat cheese

250g asparagus, cooked
but still firm, in pieces
250g green beans,
cooked but still firm
150g soft goats cheese,
grated
4 tbs olive oil
grated peel and juice of
1 lemon
1 tbs stock
2 spring onions in rings
salt

1 Mix the oil, grated lemon peel, lemon juice, and stock well and flavour with salt.
2 Add the asparagus, green beans, and spring onions and mix well.
3 Portion on to four plates, sprinkle with goats cheese.

Watercress salad with Pecorino shavings

200g watercress, leaves only
500g asparagus, cooked
but still firm, in pieces
1 red onion, in rings
1 red sweet pepper,
sliced into strips
100g hazel nuts
100g shaved pecorino
(use cheese grater to make
shavings)

For the marinade:
4 tbs maize oil
1 tsp lemon juice
1 tsp coarse mustard
1 tsp sugar

1 Blend all the ingredients for the marinade
2 Put the still warm asparagus in the marinade and marinate for
   1 hour.
3 Portion the watercress leaves on to four plates and garnish
   with the onion and the sweet pepper.
4 Take the asparagus out of the marinade and divide them with
   the nuts and the cheese over the salad.
5 Add the marinade liquid to the salad.

Spinach salad with marinated asparagus and quails' eggs

500g asparagus,
cooked, in pieces
500g new spinach
in large strips
16 fresh quails' eggs,
poached (see asparagus stock
with poached quails eggs)
100g pine nuts, roasted

For the marinade:
4 tbs maize oil
1 tsp white wine vinegar
1 tsp sugar
1 tsp coarse mustard

1 Blend the ingredients for the marinade.
2 Add the still warm pieces of asparagus and marinate for
   1 hour.
3 Portion the spinach on to four plates.
4 Lay the asparagus and the eggs on the spinach and sprinkle
   with pine nuts.
5 Sprinkle the marinade liquid over the salad.

Herb salad with asparagus and Parmesan cheese

500g asparagus,
cooked, in pieces
1 tbs chervil,
coarsely chopped
1 tbs parsley,
coarsely chopped
1 tbs watercress, chopped
100g lamb's lettuce
12 cherry tomatoes, in halves
100g shaved Parmesan cheese

For the dressing:
2 tbs olive oil
2 tbs lemon juice
sea salt

1 Mix the oil with the lemon juice and a little sea salt.
2 Spoon the dressing through the herbs and salad.
3 Lay the asparagus over the salad and garnish with the cheese and the tomatoes.

Spanish asparagus salad

500g asparagus, cooked,
but still firm, in pieces
200g small potatoes,
cooked, in slices
1 red onion, in rings
2 tomatoes, skinned, seeds
and membrane removed,
in cubes
1 red pepper, seeds removed,
sliced in strips
1 lettuce

For the marinade:
2 tbs olive oil
2 tbs maize oil
1 tsp coarse mustard
1 tsp white wine vinegar
1 tsp ginger syrup
salt

1 Blend the ingredients for the marinade well and flavour with salt.
2 Mix the marinade together with the potatoes, asparagus, onion, tomato, and pepper. Marinate for 30 minutes.
3 Cover four plates with lettuce leaves.
4 Scoop the vegetables out of the marinade and portion out on to the lettuce leaves.

Asparagus salad with strawberries and farmhouse cheese

500g asparagus, cooked,
but still firm, in pieces
½ head of frisée lettuce
150g strawberries, in halves
100g farmhouse cheese,
in slivers

To make the marinade:
2 tbs maize oil
2 tbs stock
1 tsp mustard
1 tsp white wine vinegar
50g strawberries
salt

1 Mix all the ingredients for the dressing with the hand blender.
2 Portion the salad out on to four plates. Lay the asparagus, strawberry halves and cheese on the salad.
3 Pour the dressing over the salad.

Main meal salad with asparagus, small potatoes, egg, and cheese

1kg asparagus, cooked
but still firm, in pieces
400g small potatoes,
cooked in the skin
200g cheese, diced
1 spring onion, in rings
4 hard boiled eggs, quarters
1 small bunch of chervil

For the dressing:
4 tbs olive oil
2 tbs asparagus stock
(see introduction)
1 tsp white wine vinegar
1 tsp honey
salt

1 Blend all the ingredients for the dressing and flavour with salt.
2 Mix the asparagus, small potatoes, cheese, and spring onion with the dressing and portion on to four plates.
3 Lay the eggs and the chervil sprigs on the salad.

Asparagus salad with spinach, chicken, and balsamic vinegar

500g asparagus,
cooked, in pieces
150g spinach,
400g chicken fillet, in slices
2 tbs olive oil
200g mushrooms, in slices
2 tbs balsamic vinegar
1 tbs Parmesan cheese, grated
salt and pepper

1 Season the chicken with salt and pepper, heat the oil in a pan and brown the chicken for 3 minutes.
2 Fry the mushrooms with the chicken for a moment and add the vinegar.
3 Lay the spinach on four plates and place the chicken-asparagus mixture in the middle of each plate.
4 Place the asparagus over the salad and then pour the frying liquid over it.
5 Sprinkle with cheese.

Main courses

Asparagus with parsley-egg sauce

2kg asparagus, cooked,
but still firm, in pieces of 4cm
2dl milk
8 hard boiled egg yolks,
finely mashed
200g butter
4 tbs parsley, chopped finely

1 Warm the milk and add the egg yolks. Mix well.
2 Add the butter and stir till the sauce is smooth and thick.
3 Stir the parsley into the sauce.
4 Portion the asparagus on to four plates and pour the sauce over them.

Asparagus pastry with broccoli and Kernhem cheese

4 pieces of puff pastry
200g cream cheese
200g Kernhem cheese
2 eggs
200ml cooking cream
4 broccoli florets,
cooked for 1 minute
4 asparagus spears, cooked
but still firm, in small pieces
salt and pepper
4 soufflé dishes, greased
with a little butter

1 Line the soufflé dishes with the puff pastry and prick little holes in the bottom with a fork. Preheat the oven to 190°C (374°F).

2 Blend the cheese, eggs and cooking cream. Taste to see if salt and pepper are needed.

3 Divide the broccoli and the asparagus between the dishes. Pour the egg-cheese mixture into them.

4 Place the soufflé dishes in the oven. After 10 minutes turn the heat down to 150°C (302°F) and cook the pastries in the oven for 40 minutes till done.

Asparagus risotto with mussels

400g risotto rice
200g asparagus,
cooked but still firm
2kg mussels, cooked
50g green peas,
cooked but still firm
50g new broad beans,
cooked but still firm
50g green beans,
cooked but still firm
1 onion, finely chopped
1 tbs butter for frying the onion
1l vegetable stock, hot
25g butter
100g Grana Padano or
Parmesan cheese, grated
salt and pepper

1   Heat the butter and sauté the onion. Add the risotto and keep stirring till the rice is glazed.
2   Pour some hot stock over the rice and only add new stock when the liquid has been absorbed. Keep stirring well. Repeat this till the rice is done. This will take about 20 minutes.
3   Stir in the asparagus, peas, broad beans, green beans, butter and cheese. Add salt and pepper to taste.
4   Set aside 12 mussels, complete with shells. Remove the rest from their shells. Stir these through the rice.
5   Portion the risotto on to four plates and garnish each plate with 3 mussels in their shells.

Millefeuille with wolf fish and asparagus

500g wolf fish, in pieces
12 asparagus spears,
cooked but still firm
4 pieces of puff pastry,
defrosted, cut in
half lengthwise
1 egg yolk
400g spinach
olive oil

1 Preheat the oven to 200°C (392°F). Cut the asparagus into pieces with the same length as the puff pastry.
2 Paint the egg yolk onto the puff pastry. Prick holes into the puff pastry with a fork. Bake in the oven for 4 minutes till it is brown and crisp.
3 Sprinkle salt over the wolf fish and brown nicely in olive oil. Cook for 4 minutes on a low flame.
4 Stir-fry the spinach in a little oil till it begins to shrink. Lay the spinach in the middle of each of the 4 plates.
5 Place a piece of puff pastry on the spinach with the asparagus and the fish on top of that. Cover with the remaining pieces of puff pastry.

Caramelized asparagus with red mullet and white wine sauce

1kg asparagus, peeled,
in pieces cut at an angle
8 red mullet fillets
Oil for frying
1 tbs butter
1 tbs sugar
Juice of 1 lemon

For the white wine sauce:
½ onion, finely chopped
½ large carrot, finely chopped
¼ stick of blanched celery,
finely chopped
1 tbs olive oil
380ml concentrated fish stock
200ml dry white wine
200ml cooking cream
pepper and salt

For the parsley oil:
½ bunch of parsley
1 clove of garlic
4 tbs olive oil
salt

1. To make the sauce, fry the vegetables in oil. Add the concentrated fish stock, the wine, and the cream. Simmer for 30 minutes, sieve the sauce and season with salt and pepper. Reduce the sauce if you prefer it to be thicker.
2. Grind all the ingredients for the parsley oil fine with the hand blender and add salt to taste.
3. Gently fry the mullet in the oil with the red side facing down.
4. Turn the mullet over and fry for about 4 minutes till done.
5. Melt the butter in another pan and stir-fry the asparagus in 5 minutes till they are cooked but still firm.
6. Sprinkle the sugar over the asparagus and caramelize.
7. Add the lemon juice and stir well.
8. Portion the asparagus on to four plates. Lay the fish on the asparagus.
9. Pour sauce around the asparagus and fish and then drizzle the parsley oil over them.

Veal au gratin

4 veal steaks of about
130g cut in half
8 slices taleggio
(Italian cheese)
500g asparagus,
cooked but still firm
2 head of puk choi,
in large pieces
1 tbs butter
1 tbs oil
salt

1 Sprinkle the veal steaks with a little salt and brown nicely in butter. Then simmer for about 3 minutes.
2 Lay a slice of cheese on each steak. Brown in the oven for 1 minute at 150°C (302°F) till the cheese starts to melt.
3 Stir-fry the pak choi in a little oil: make sure it remains crispy.
4 Portion the vegetables onto 4 plates. Put a veal steak on top, then a few asparagus and then the other steak.

Tip: delicious together with Marsala sauce (see lamb tongue salad and asparagus with Marsala sauce).

Fillet of salmon with asparagus, spring vegetables, and Noilly-Prat sauce

4 pieces of salmon of about
130g with skin
500g asparagus
100g mange touts
100g green beans
salt

For the Noilly Prat sauce:
½ onion, finely cut
½ large carrot, finely cut
¼ stick of blanched celery,
finely cut
1 tbs olive oil
380ml concentrated fish stock
200ml Noilly Prat
(or dry sherry)
200ml cream
pepper and salt

1 To make the sauce, fry the vegetables in the oil. Add the concentrated stock, the Noilly Prat, and the cream. Simmer for 30 minutes; sieve the sauce and season with pepper and salt. Reduce the sauce if you prefer it thicker.

2 Cook the vegetables, but make sure they are still firm (asparagus 10-15 minutes, green beans 10-15 minutes, the mange tout 3 to 4 minutes).

3 Warm a small smoking oven to a moderate heat using beech shavings.

4 Sprinkle the fillet of salmon with salt and put them in the preheated smoking oven. Smoke the salmon for about 10 minutes till it is still pink on the inside and smoked on the outside.

5 Mix the mange tout, green beans, and asparagus and portion this on to four plates.

6 Lay the salmon fillet on top and pour the sauce around the salmon and the vegetables.

first. Turn it over and fry for about 5 minutes on the skin side till it is nice and pink inside.

Asparagus and goats cheese soufflé with rocket sauce

500g asparagus, cooked but
still firm, in small pieces
400g soft goat cheese
4 eggs
100g mature cheese, grated
1dl cooking cream
soufflé dishes,
greased with butter

For the rocket sauce:
200ml asparagus stock
(see the introduction
to this book)
200ml cream
2 tbs white wine
50g pine nuts, roasted
1 small bunch of rocket,
finely cut
salt

1 Preheat the oven to 150°C (302°F).
2 To make the sauce, heat and reduce the stock, cream, and wine to half. Add the pine nuts and rocket. Make sure it is really warm and season with salt.
3 Mix the goat cheese, eggs, mature cheese, and cream in a food processor or use a hand blender.
4 Fill the soufflé dishes with the cheese mixture.
5 Portion out the asparagus amongst the dishes.
6 Cook the soufflé in the oven for 40 minutes. Serve immediately.

Wild rice with asparagus and halibut

250g wild rice
1kg asparagus, cooked
but still firm, in pieces
500 g halibut
1 tbs butter
1 shallot, finely chopped
½ tbs olive oil
2 tbs white wine
3 tbs Parmesan cheese, grated
salt

1 Cook the wild rice according to the instructions on the packet.
2 Salt the halibut and brown it nicely in the butter. Cook the fish for another 5 minutes, take it out of the pan and keep it warm.
3 Fry the shallot in the oil and add the white wine. Put the shallot and the wine in the pan in which you fried the fish.
4 Let the mixture cook for a minute, then stir it through the rice with the asparagus and the Parmesan.
5 Portion on to four plates and lay the fish on top.

Tip: Tasty with a mixed salad.

Pasta dish with stir-fried shrimps and asparagus

400g pasta
200g large shrimps, peeled,
rinsed and dried
1kg asparagus, peeled
in pieces and cut an angle
Oil for stir-frying
1 piece of ginger, grated
1 tbs dry sherry
1 tbs soy sauce
2 tsp sesame oil
2 tbs maize oil
1 small bunch dill

1 Pour a little oil in the wok and stir-fry the asparagus for 4 minutes.
2 Add the ginger, sherry, soy sauce, the two kinds of oil and heat well.
3 Add the shrimps and mix well till everything is thoroughly warmed.
4 Mix with the pasta or serve the pasta separately.
5 Garnish with sprigs of dill.

Asparagus with lamb fillet and spinach

4 lamb fillets of about 130g
500g asparagus, peeled,
in large pieces
400g spinach
50g bacon bits
3 lbs white wine
1 twig rosemary
½ large carrot in pieces
1 shallot, finely cut
1 clove of garlic, crushed
300g beef stock
Honey
oil for frying
salt

1 Preheat the oven to 80°C (176°F). Sprinkle the lamb fillets with salt and fry them quickly on both sides in a little oil. Take them out of the pan.
2 Fry the bacon bits till crispy: add the wine and put the bacon bits and the wine in a baking dish.
3 Add the rosemary, carrot, shallot, and garlic. Fill the dish with stock till it is 1/3 full and lay the lambs fillets on top.
4 Cover the baking dish with foil and put in the oven for 30 minutes.
5 Stir-fry the asparagus in a little oil or butter till they are light-brown.
6 Take the baking dish out of the oven. Set the lamb fillets apart, keep them warm.
7 Sieve the liquid and reduce to a sauce. Stir in a little honey.
6 Stir-fry the spinach and put it in the middle of the 4 plates. Portion the asparagus onto the plates. Cut the lamb fillet in slices and lay these on the asparagus. Serve the sauce separately.

Stuffed veal with Cognac sauce

4 veal cutlets of about 125g,
tenderised
6 asparagus spears, cooked,
but still firm in halves
8 sage leaves, 4 in strips
4 slices Parma ham
Butter or oil for frying
salt
4 cocktail prickers

For the sauce:
½ onion, finely cut
¼ large carrot, finely cut
¼ stick of blanched celery
finely cut
½ blanched celery stick,
finely cut
380ml concentrated stock
200ml red wine
200ml cream
2 tbs Cognac
1 tbs olive oil
pepper and salt

1 To make the sauce, gently fry the onion, carrot and blanched celery in olive oil. Add the concentrated stock, red wine, cream and cognac and simmer for half an hour. Keep separately or reduce if you prefer a thicker sauce.
2 Preheat the over to 125°C (257°F).
3 On each veal cutlet, lay a sage leaf, a slice of Parma ham, and 4 halved asparagus spears. Roll them up and fasten with a cocktail pick.
4 Brown the rolls in butter or oil and put in the oven for another 5 minutes till cooked.
5 Cut the meat at an angle so the asparagus and the sage are visible and portion on to the plates. Add the rest of the asparagus, pour the sauce around the asparagus and garnish with the strips of sage.

Asparagus with ham off the bone and scrambled eggs

400g ham off the bone,
in thin slices,
warmed in the oven
1kg asparagus,
cooked but
still firm
4 eggs
2 tbs cooking cream
chives for garnishing
salt and pepper

1 Beat the eggs with the cooking cream and a little salt and pepper. Scramble the eggs in the butter with a spoon.
2 Portion the asparagus on to four plates. Lay the ham partly on the asparagus, partly next to them. Lay the scrambled eggs next to the ham.
3 Garnish with cut chives.

Stir-fried steak with mixed vegetables

400g steak, in slices
500g white asparagus,
in pieces of 4cm
500g green asparagus,
hard underside removed,
in pieces of 4cm
1 courgette, in slices of 4cm
1 red sweet pepper, in slices
1 small bunch of chives,
finely cut
oil or butter for frying
salt and pepper

1 Heat the oil or butter and stir-fry the vegetables till they are cooked but still firm.
2 Using another pan, heat butter or oil till it is very hot.
3 Sprinkle the steak with pepper and salt. Fry the slices brown quickly, first on one side and then on the other.
4 Portion the meat and the vegetables on to four plates and garnish with chives.

Delicious when served with a baguette

Tenderloin with oyster mushrooms, asparagus and tomato coulis

4 tenderloin steaks
of about 130g
500g asparagus, peeled,
in pieces of 5cm
2 tbs white wine
100ml tomato coulis
100g oyster mushrooms
1 spring onion in rings
oil for frying
salt and pepper

For the tomato coulis:
500g tomatoes
100ml dry white wine
200ml vegetable stock

1   To make the tomato coulis, cook the tomatoes for 15 minutes in the wine and the stock. Purée the tomato mixture with the hand blender. Sieve the coulis and season with salt and pepper.
2   Sprinkle the steaks with salt and pepper and fry them in a pan until they have reached the desired degree of cooking.
3   Fry the asparagus for 3 minutes till light brown.
4   Fry the mushrooms gently.
5   Lay the asparagus in the centre of each plate and place the oyster mushrooms on top. Pour the coulis around the asparagus and garnish with spring onion.

Asparagus wok dish with pistachio nuts

500g white asparagus,
peeled, in pieces cut
at an angle
500g green asparagus,
hard underside removed,
in pieces cut at an angle
2 spring onions, in rings
2 cloves of garlic, crushed
100g unsalted pistachio nuts
1 tbs maize oil

For the sauce:
1 tbs soy sauce
1 tbs vegetable stock
1 tbs ginger, freshly grated

1 Heat the oil in a wok and stir-fry the asparagus, spring onions, and garlic for 5 minutes.
2 Mix the ingredients for the sauce. Add the vegetables and bring to the boil while stirring.
3 Turn of the heat source; mix the nuts through the dish and let it stand for a minute.

Great with pasta.

Aubergine rolls with asparagus and goat cheese

1 aubergine in 8 thin slices
12 asparagus spears, sliced
with a peeler into slivers
200g goat cheese
2 sprigs of rosemary;
the needles
2 tbs olive oil
Juice of ½ lemon
1 tsp sea salt
50g rocket

For the sweet pepper coulis:
2 sweet peppers, red
100ml dry white wine
200ml vegetable stock
Salt and pepper

1 Preheat the oven to 200°C (392°F).
2 Warm the oil, put the rosemary in it and let it steep for 2 hours.
3 Add the lemon juice, sea salt, and the slices of aubergine. Steep for another 20 minutes.
4 Mix the rocket with the slices of aubergine and crumble the cheese over it.
5 In the mean time, make the sweet pepper coulis by cooking the sweet peppers in the wine and the stock. Mash with the hand blender. Sieve the coulis and season with salt and pepper.
6 Take the aubergine out of the marinade, pat it dry (keep the marinade) and put the slices under the grill or on the grill plate for a little while.
7 Divide the asparagus mix over the aubergines and roll them up nicely. Heat them in the oven for about 2 minutes.
8 Put 2 rolls on each plate. Pour a little marinade liquid over the rolls.

Asparagus and prawn bake

500g asparagus, cooked but
still firm, in pieces
200g prawns, skinned, slightly
fried, in pieces
500g mashed potatoes
100g cheese, grated
1 small bunch parsley,
coarsely chopped

1 Preheat the oven at 200°C (392°F)
2 Mix the prawn and the asparagus through the mashed
   potatoes.
3 Grease an oven dish with butter. Put the potato mixture in the
   dish and sprinkle with cheese.
4 Bake the mashed potatoes au gratin for 10 minutes. Garnish
   with parsley.

Scampi with stir-fried asparagus and marsh samphire

20 scampi
1kg asparagus, peeled,
in pieces cut an angle
100g marsh samphire
2 tbs olive oil

1 Sir-fry the asparagus in 1 tbs oil till they are cooked but still firm and golden brown.
2 Add the marsh samphire at the last minute.
3 Fry the scampi in the remaining oil.
4 Divide the asparagus and the marsh samphire over the 4 plates. Lay the scampi on them. Serve with white wine sauce (see recipe Asparagus with red mullet and white wine sauce).

Tip: marsh samphire tastes very salty and has a substantial bite to it. If you immerse it in boiling water, the taste and flavour will become milder.

Asparagus quiche with smoked trout

200g smoked trout fillet,
in pieces
500g asparagus, cooked but
still firm, in small pieces
6 slices of puff pastry, rolled
out to make a piece
the same size as the
quiche mould
1 tbs breadcrumbs
3 eggs
200g cream cheese
2 dl cream
1 tbs dill, finely chopped
1 quiche mould

1 Preheat the oven to 200°C (392°F). Cover the quiche mould with the puff pastry, also the wall.
2 Prick little holes in it with a fork.
3 Lay the trout at the bottom and place the asparagus on top.
4 Beat the eggs, cheese, cream, and dill together with the hand blender till it becomes an even mixture. Fill the quiche mould with it.
5 Place the quiche in the middle of the oven and bake it for 10 minutes. Set the oven to 160°C (320°F) and bake the quiche for another 30 minutes till it is cooked. The filling should be completely set.

The quiche can be eaten warm or cold. Tasty with a green salad.

Asparagus with farmhouse cheese and parsley-oil

1kg asparagus, cooked but
still firm, in pieces of 4cm
200g farmhouse cheese,
in cubes
2 hard boiled eggs,
finely chopped
½ bunch of parsley,
finely chopped

For the parsley-oil:
½ bunch parsley
1 clove garlic, crushed
5 tbs olive oil
salt

1 Put the ingredients for the parsley-oil in a bowl. Blend them with the hand blender till they are very fine and season with salt.
2 Mix the asparagus with the cheese and eggs.
3 Portion on to four plates and then sprinkle with the chopped parsley.
4 Pour the oil around the dish.

Risotto with asparagus and spring vegetables

400g risotto rice
500g asparagus, cooked
but still firm, in pieces
200g green beans, cooked
but still firm
200g mange touts, cooked
but still firm
1 shallot, finely cut
½ tbs butter
1l vegetable stock, hot
1 tbs white wine
2 tbs sun-dried tomatoes,
in slices
4 tbs Parmesan cheese, grated
pepper and salt

1 Fry the shallot in the butter until glazed and then add the rice.
2 Stir-fry the rice until glazed and then add a tablespoon of hot stock together with the wine.
3 Stir the rice till all the liquid has been absorbed and then add more stock. Keep repeating this till the rice is cooked (about 20 minutes).
4 Add the asparagus, mange touts, green beans and tomatoes. Season with pepper and salt.
5 Stir in the cheese and portion on to four plates.

Filo pastry filled with asparagus, sage, and ham

8 slices of filo pastry, defrosted
1kg asparagus, cooked but
still firm, in pieces
8 slices of cooked ham,
in slices
½ small bunch of sage, sliced
1 egg, beaten

1 Preheat the oven to 225°C (437°F).
2 Paint the 4 pieces of pastry with egg. Lay another slice of pastry on each slice and also paint this with egg.
3 Cut the pieces in half and fill them with asparagus, ham and sage.
4 Fold the pastry into 8 parcels.
5 Bake parcels in the oven for 10 minutes until golden brown.

Poached bergylt fillet with asparagus

600g bergylt fillet
1kg asparagus, peeled,
in pieces of 4cm
1 onion, finely chopped
1 tbs olive oil
200g green peas,
fresh or frozen
2 tbs white wine
250g fish stock
1 small bunch of dill
salt

1 Fry the onion in oil (in an ordinary pan)
2 Add the green peas and lay the asparagus on top.
3 Lay the bergylt on the bed of vegetables and pour the white
   wine and the stock over the fish.
4 Add a little salt and cook for approximately 15 minutes in a
   closed pan.
5 Serve the fish on the bed of vegetables and garnish with dill
   twigs.

Lamb cutlets with asparagus, shiitake mushrooms and mint sauce

12 lamb cutlets
1 tbs butter or oil
500g white asparagus,
cooked but still firm, in pieces
500g green asparagus,
cooked but still firm, in pieces
100g shiitake mushrooms
salt and pepper

For the sauce:
½ onion, finely chopped
½ large carrot, finely chopped
¼ stick blanched celery,
finely chopped
1 tbs olive oil
380ml concentrated stock
200ml red wine
200ml cream
½ bunch mint, finely cut
pepper and salt

1 To make the sauce, fry the vegetables in the oil. Add the concentrated stock, the wine and the cream. Add the mint. Simmer for about 30 minutes, sieve the sauce, and season with pepper and salt. Reduce the sauce if you prefer it thicker.
2 Sprinkle the cutlets with salt and pepper and fry them for approx. 1 minute on either side in butter or oil.
3 Take them out of the pan and allow to rest in a warm place.
4 Portion asparagus on to four plates and place the cutlets on top.
5 Fry the mushrooms for a short while in a dry frying pan. Lay them on the plates and pour the sauce around them.

Tartlet of preserved duck drumsticks and asparagus

6 duck drumsticks
3 tbs oil
1l goose fat (poulterer)
1 bay leaf
1 tsp sea salt
4 asparagus spears, peeled,
in small cubes
½ small bunch of parsley,
finely chopped
1 sweet pepper, red,
in small blocks
200g green beans,
in small pieces
pepper and salt

1 Preheat the oven to 125°C (257°F). Sprinkle the drumsticks with pepper and salt and bake them in one tbs oil till they are nicely browned.
2 Heat the goose fat, add the bay leaf and the salt and pour into a heat-resistant dish.
3 Lay the drumsticks in the dish and put in the oven for 5 hours.
4 When the duck is well cooked, let it cool a bit; then take the meat off the bone.
5 Add 1 tbs asparagus cubes and the parsley and mix well.
6 With a cutter, make tartlets out of the meat mixture and then heat them up in the oven.
7 Heat the rest of the oil and stir fry the other vegetables till they are cooked but still firm.
8 Put the tartlet in the middle of the plates and arrange the vegetables around it.

Appetizers

Crostini make the perfect base for appetizers as they're both tasty and easy to eat. If you're after an alternative, you can use Melba toast, various kinds of toasted bread, or rye bread instead.

Crostini with smoked salmon, asparagus, and dill

makes approximately
10 crostini
½ baguette, in slices cut
at an angle
2 tbs olive oil
Coarse sea salt
100g smoked salmon,
in 10 slices
4 asparagus spears, cooked,
in pieces
4 dill twigs

1 Preheat the oven to 200°C (392°F).
2 Spread the olive oil over the baguette slices and sprinkle with sea salt.
3 Bake the bread in 5 minutes nicely brown and crusty in the oven.
4 Put the salmon on the slices of bread, which is now called crostini. Lay the asparagus over the crostini and garnish with dill.

Crostini with asparagus, mascarpone and egg

10 crostini
(see previous recipe)
6 tbs mascarpone
2 boiled eggs, finely mashed
4 asparagus spears, cooked
but still firm, in small pieces
1 tbs spring onion,
finely chopped
1 tbs parsley, chopped
½ sweet pepper, red,
in slices
salt and pepper

1 Mix the mascarpone, eggs, asparagus, spring onion, and parsley well. Season with salt and pepper.
2 Spread the mixture on the crostini.
3 Garnish with the sweet pepper.

Filled eggs with asparagus mousse

5 hard boiled eggs, in halves
2dl white wine,
reduced to half
4 asparagus spears, cooked
but still firm, in pieces
1 slice of ham, in slices
1 twig of parsley

1 Take the yolk carefully out of the eggs. Mix it with the white wine.
2 Blend in the asparagus.
3 Fill the eggs with the mixture. Divide the slices of ham and garnish with the parsley.

Crostini with scampi, asparagus, and garlic parsley dressing

10 crostini (see recipe p.159)
4 green asparagus spears,
cooked for 4 minutes,
in small pieces
4 white asparagus spears,
cooked but still firm,
in small pieces
10 scampi, fried

For the dressing:
1 tsp mustard
1 tsp honey
2 tbs stock
1 egg yolk
1 tsp white wine vinegar
2 cloves of garlic, crushed
½ small bunch of
parsley, chopped
3dl maize oil

1 To make the dressing, mix the mustard, honey, stock, egg yolk, vinegar, garlic, and parsley with the hand blender. Pour in the maize oil drop by drop till the dressing starts to bind.
2 On each crostini, place two pieces of green asparagus, 2 pieces of white asparagus, and a scampi on top. Sprinkle with a little dressing.

Crostini with asparagus, feta, and sun-dried tomato

10 crostini (see recipe p.159)
100g feta, in cubes
10 sun-dried tomatoes
4 white asparagus, cooked
in small cubes
10 lettuce leaves
4 blades of chives,
finely chopped

1 Mix the feta, tomato, and asparagus together.
2 Lay a lettuce leaf on the crostini and place the cheese mixture on top.
3 Garnish with the chives.

Crostini with marinated mussels and asparagus

10 crostini (see recipe p.159)
20 mussels, cooked,
shells removed
4 asparagus spears, cooked,
in small pieces
10 lettuce leaves

For the mussel marinade:
2 tbs maize oil
1 tsp mustard
juice of ½ lemon
2 sprigs of parsley,
finely chopped

1 Mix the ingredients for the marinade well.
2 Pour the marinade over the mussels and marinate for 1 hour.
3 Take the mussels out of the marinade and pat them dry. Keep the marinade.
4 Lay a lettuce leaf on each crostini. Place the asparagus and the mussels on top.
5 Pour a little marinade over the crostini.

Crostini with shrimps, asparagus, and tomato

10 crostini (see recipe p.159)
100g shrimps
2 asparagus spears, cooked
but still firm, in pieces cut
at an angle
100g lamb's lettuce
1 tomato, pulp removed

To make the dressing:
2 tbs olive oil
2 tbs maize oil
1 egg yolk
1 tsp mustard
1 tsp white wine vinegar
1 tsp honey
2 tomatoes, skinned, in pieces

1 With the exception of the oil, purée the ingredients for the dressing in a food processor.
2 Add the oil drop by drop till the dressing binds. Season with salt.
3 Place the lettuce, shrimps, asparagus, and tomato cubes on the crostini. Spoon the dressing over the crostini.

Crostini with Pastrami and asparagus

10 crostini (see recipe p.159)
200g pastrami, in thin slices
4 asparagus spears,
cooked, in slices

1 Place the slices of pastrami on the crostini and then arrange the asparagus slices over them.

Crostini with pea purée and asparagus

10 crostini (see recipe p.159)
100g green peas, fresh
or frozen, cooked
4 asparagus spears, peeled,
cooked but still firm,
in pieces of 4cm.
1 tbs olive oil
salt

1 Make a purée with the green peas and the olive oil. Season with salt.
2 Spread the crostini with the purée and arrange the asparagus pieces on top.

Filled eggs with ham mousse and asparagus

100g cooked ham
2dl white,
wine reduced to half
5 hard boiled eggs, in halves
4 white asparagus spears,
cooked, in pieces
4 green asparagus spears,
cooked, in pieces

1 Put the ham with the white wine in a food processor and process until it becomes a mousse.
2 Take the yolk out of the eggs and mix with the mousse.
3 Fill the egg halves with the mixture.
4 Arrange the asparagus over the eggs.

Asparagus rolled in salmon

100g smoked salmon,
in 4 slices
4 asparagus spears,
in pieces of 4cm

1 Place an equal number of asparagus pieces on to each slice of salmon.
2 Roll the slices up.

Tip: asparagus rolled in roast beef or ham is also very tasty.

Index